# LION VS. HYENA CLAN

BY NATHAN SOMMER

BELLWETHER MEDIA • MINNEAPOLIS, MN

T0020279

Torque brims with excitement perfect for thrill-seekers of all kinds. Discover daring survival skills, explore uncharted worlds, and marvel at mighty engines and extreme sports. In *Torque* books, anything can happen. Are you ready?

Library of Congress Cataloging-in-Publication Data

Title: Lion vs. Hyena Clan / by Nathan Sommer.
Other titles: Lion versus hyena clan
Description: Minneapolis, MN : Bellwether Media, Inc., 2020. | Series: Torque: animal battles | Includes bibliographical references and index. | Audience: Ages 7-12 | Audience: Grades 3-7 | Summary: ""Amazing photography accompanies engaging information about the fighting abilities of lions and hyenas. The combination of high-interest subject matter and light text is intended for students in grades 3 through 7"–Provided by publisher"– Provided by publisher.
Identifiers: LCCN 2019031892 (print) | LCCN 2019031893 (ebook) | ISBN 9781644871591 (library binding) | ISBN 9781618918390 (ebook)
Subjects: LCSH: Lion–Juvenile literature. | Hyenas–Juvenile literature.
Classification: LCC QL737.C23 S5838 2020 (print) | LCC QL737.C23 (ebook) | DDC 599.757–dc23
LC record available at https://lccn.loc.gov/2019031892
LC ebook record available at https://lccn.loc.gov/2019031893

Editor: Christina Leaf       Designer: Andrea Schneider

Printed in the United States of America, North Mankato, MN.

# TABLE OF CONTENTS

# THE COMPETITORS

Few **habitats** are tougher than African **savannas**. Within them, lions are known as the king of beasts.

But these big cats are often challenged by sly hyena **clans**. Living in groups as big as 80, hyenas are world-class hunters. It is a constant battle for savanna dominance between these two **predators**!

Lions can eat as much as 75 pounds (34 kilograms) of meat in one sitting!

Lions are the world's second-largest cats. They have long bodies and large heads. Scruffy manes surround the faces of males.

Lions live in groups called prides. Prides usually have around 15 lions. They often hunt and eat together. The ferocious **carnivores** take whatever meat they find. They like to forcefully steal food from other predators like hyenas.

# AFRICAN LION PROFILE

## LENGTH
**UP TO 7 FEET (2.1 METERS)**

0          5 FEET          10 FEET

## WEIGHT
**UP TO 500 POUNDS (227 KILOGRAMS)**

## HABITAT

PLAINS          SAVANNAS          WOODLANDS

## AFRICAN LION RANGE

■ RANGE

# SPOTTED HYENA PROFILE

**LENGTH**
UP TO 6.6 FEET
(2 METERS)

**WEIGHT**
UP TO
180 POUNDS
(82 KILOGRAMS)

0        4 FEET        8 FEET

**HABITAT**

PLAINS     SAVANNAS     WOODLANDS     DESERTS

**SPOTTED HYENA RANGE**

■ RANGE

Hyenas are tough creatures. They have long legs and muscular necks and shoulders that can carry **prey** over far distances. Spotted hyenas are the most common. Brown spots cover their tan fur.

Hyenas are highly social. They talk to each other with laughs and yells. These can be heard from miles away!

## HYENAS VS. HUMANS

Most humans do not like sharing habitats with hyenas. Hyena clans often kill livestock, fight humans, and steal food from stores!

# SECRET WEAPONS

MANE

Several **adaptations** protect lions from danger. Furry manes guard males' necks while fighting. Yellow-gold fur helps **camouflage** them in tall grass.

# SECRET WEAPONS

**HYENA**

| SUPER SMELL | SUPER HEARING | SPEED AND ENERGY | POWERFUL JAWS |

Hyenas use super senses to their **advantage**. They can hear enemies coming from 6 miles (9.6 kilometers) away! Strong noses smell nearby animals before they are even in sight.

MANE

CAMOUFLAGE FUR

SHARP CLAWS

SHARP TEETH

LION

Lion paws have 18 razor-sharp claws. These can be more than 1 inch (2.5 centimeters) long. Thumb-like toes hold down enemies during attacks.

Hyenas make up what they lack in size with speed and energy. They can run up to 40 miles (64.3 kilometers) per hour for miles at a time!

# HYENA TOP SPEED

40 MPH (64.3 KM/H)

28 MPH (45 KM/H)

FOR SEVERAL MILES

0    1 MILE    2 MILES    3 MILES

FOR ABOUT 330 FEET (100 METERS)

0    2000 FEET    4000 FEET    6000 FEET

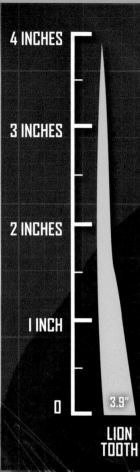

4 INCHES

3 INCHES

2 INCHES

1 INCH

0          3.9"

LION
TOOTH

Enemies fear lions' big bites. The beasts can
open their mouths almost 1 foot (30 centimeters)
wide! Inside, their sharp **canine teeth** can be
3.9 inches (10 centimeters) long.

Hyenas trade sharp teeth for powerful bites. Their molars are strong enough to crush horns and hooves. They can break bones with just one bite!

# ATTACK MOVES

Lions are built to hunt. They **stalk** foes from hidden locations. Then they catch them off-guard with rush attacks.

Hyenas' teamwork allows them to take down large animals. Clans team up to drag enemies to the ground. Then they use strong jaws to tear them apart bite after bite.

Lions leap on enemies to take them down.
They pounce at necks for a fast takedown.
Large, sharp claws tear into foes as needed.

Hyenas' speed and energy is enough to run most enemies into **exhaustion**. They aim for the stomach to finish the job. These hunters then eat their prey!

# READY, FIGHT!

A hungry male lion sees five hyenas eating a zebra. It is outnumbered, but this does not matter at mealtime!

The lion claws and injures the clan leader. It bites another who sneaks up from behind. This scares away the others. Hyenas win in larger numbers. But today the lion used size and strength to steal a feast!

# GLOSSARY

**adaptations**—changes in animals over time that make them better able to hunt and survive

**advantage**—something an animal has or can do better than their enemy

**camouflage**—to blend in with the surroundings

**canine teeth**—long, pointed teeth that are often the sharpest in the mouth

**carnivores**—animals that only eat meat

**clans**—groups of hyenas that live and hunt together

**exhaustion**—a state of being very mentally and physically weak due to working too hard

**habitats**—the homes or areas where animals prefer to live

**predators**—animals that hunt other animals for food

**prey**—animals that are hunted by other animals for food

**savannas**—flat grasslands in Africa with very few trees

**stalk**—to follow closely and quietly

# TO LEARN MORE

## AT THE LIBRARY

Gagne, Tammy. *Lions: Built for the Hunt*. North Mankato, Minn.: Capstone Press, 2016.

Polinsky, Paige V. *Spotted Hyena: Cackling Carnivore of the Savanna*. Minneapolis, Minn.: Abdo Publishing, 2017.

Sommer, Nathan. *Grizzly Bear vs. Wolf Pack*. Minneapolis, Minn.: Bellwether Media, 2020.

## ON THE WEB

# FACTSURFER

Factsurfer.com gives you a safe, fun way to find more information.

1. Go to www.factsurfer.com

2. Enter "lion vs. hyena clan" into the search box and click 🔍.

3. Select your book cover to see a list of related web sites.

# INDEX

The images in this book are reproduced through the courtesy of: Eric Isselee, front cover (lion); Daniel-Alvarez, front cover (hyena); LeonP, p. 4; John Michael Vosloo, p. 5; Pablo77, pp. 6-7; J. Natayo, p. 9; Ibad Ahmed, p. 10; Independent Birds, p. 11 (hyena); subin pumsom, p. 11 (weapon 1, 2); Jandrie Lombard, p. 11 (weapon 3); Vickey Chauhan, p. 11 (weapon 4); znm, p. 12 (lion); PHOTOCERO Michal Bednarek, p. 12 (weapon 1); Joe McDonald, p. 12 (weapon 2); Edwin Butter, p. 12 (weapon 3); photoshooter2015, p. 12 (weapon 4); pchoui, p. 13; Elana Erasmus, p. 14; Tom Strudley, p. 15; AndrewGreen, p. 16; Linda Marie Caldwell, pp. 17, 20-21 (back hyenas); GomezDavid, p. 18; Albie Venter, p. 19; Ali Al-Awartany, pp. 20-21 (lion); Mark Dumbleton, p. 21 (front hyena).